Things I Can't Tell My Therapist

A Chapbook: What I Should Have Said

Emily Andrews

Made with ❤ on the BookLeaf Publishing Platform
www.bookleafpub.in
www.bookleafpub.com

*To my mother— thank you for raising me strong,
and always making me feel like somebody. You
are everything I hope to be.*

Acknowledgement

I would like to express the deepest gratitude to my family for always lifting me up when I fall, and for allowing me to use our living room as a public poetry reading. You all are the lights of my life, and the reason behind my every smile. To know you is to know fortune.

I would also like to extend a thank you to my dearest friend "Sparkles" — you made it so I could write again.

Preface

I have always been vulnerable in my poetry. And I believe this is what makes poetry such an ambiguous art form. The common throughline we hear about poetry in grade school is, "it means whatever you interpret it to mean", and that is something I have tried to achieve with this project. I have taken the stereotypical therapy session (or series of sessions) and turned it into one work of all the things people may find themselves too guarded to talk about. We can have the most beautiful families and still have hurt that stems from those interpersonal relationships, and it is absolutely important to address that. All experiences are real and valid in the way you experienced them—they matter to you in the way you interpreted them. Giving ourselves the space to feel those feelings can give birth to a myriad of beautiful things—I hope this chapbook is one of them.

New Patient Paperwork

I scheduled my first appointment when I
found myself chasing a shadow—
like a whisper, or fog on a breeze,
the person I used to be, lives in the corners of
my eyes,
just out of reach—disappears before I am ever
able to really see her,
and she's screaming,
the type of scream that awakes primal panic
in your chest—
begets benevolence—
Desperation is the cruelest captor,
and she lives entombed in Him,
like nothing more than a silhouette,
a memory,
trapped in His catacombs, surrounded by
walls of her own bones—
this fun-house wasn't fun at all,
each mirror shows her a different flaw,
and I am at a loss.

But there is no space for that on the intake
form—

so I check anxiety,
depression too,
and hope that's enough to bring me back to
you.

"What Are You Thinking About?"

When we fall asleep,
where do we go?
swirling, twirling, tumbling down,
and evermore down—
through the velvet black
whose iridescent fingers coil inside of your
chest—
catch your breath,
and keep
it

                        a secret—

like the loose end of a storied string,
you cling to your life,
beginning and ending as Atropos' plaything
and your mother's tortured offspring—
you long for what this life could never bring,
and beg to keep
it

                        a secret—

Life's last straw slips your grip, and you give
way—

breathless and buried,
falling through time and every memory of
doors left open that should have been closed,
both long before and long after,
you found your way—
a road map written in foreign script,
all that is left to depict,
the light at the end of this labyrinth,

you are the only one brave enough, please—
keep
it

                a secret—

When we fall asleep,
where do we go?
Your imagination's figment of fingers, are
fixed around a key,
your mind's soliloquy takes center stage—
commands attention from you and them—
the fourth dimension,
a state of consciousness—
you've met your prophetess in your own
consequence—
and yet here you are

Godless,
a
secret

                              keep it.

"Do You Have Friends There?"

rest in peace to the person I thought I knew,
and let their transgressions perfect hospital
corners on the edges of flat sheets
until they learn what it means to be the
company you keep—
reap what you sow, and choke on a heavy
handed metaphor you were never given the
privilege to read,
maybe that is why I could never finish the
poem you commissioned me—
my pen knew better than to waste ink and the
words that fill me—
Вы это сила- vy eto
silla

a far away God sings to me—"you are
power"—and I am,
filled to the point of bursting with words and
power and every other thing that you are
afraid of,
and afraid to be,

Вы это сила
but you keep praying to your omniscient God
to take out your tongue,
render you mute, break your fingers black
and blue—
anything to hide this version of you that eats
away at all of the fruit a benevolent God
bares for you,
so rest in peace to the person I thought I
knew—
perfect your hospital corners and cottage core
your house to death
until it mirrors the tomb that lives inside of
you,
and may that be enough
to forever quiet your truth.

Journal Entry #1

Doc told me that I should try journaling
when I have feelings that confuse me—
so, here I am,
in the dark,
by the light of a Roku TV,
writing about what confuses me.

I'd like to say it was something deep—
introspective,
but I can't seem to shake the polarity of an
image,
between me,
in the light of a TV,
and every poet before me,
leaning over a single wicked flame, trying to
discern just what it all means—

the tightness in our chests,
and the world view we can only explain in
meter and feet,
that confuses me— having so much to say but
only being able to muster, "I'm sad",
unless someone thinks to give me a pen—
maybe I could tell you then.

"Do You Want Children?"

To The Daughter I Cannot Have,

I wish they taught us different subjects in
school—
like how to balance a checkbook, draw a plot
plan, and not get turned upside
down—pockets shaken out by Lenders and all
of their owe,
so well intentioned expenses—

you leave emptier than you came,
broke,
then broker than a joke that no one can
afford to laugh at, because their lungs and
tongues and laughters are lent out to now,
and ever-after.
I wish they taught us different subjects in
school—
Columbus sailed the ocean blue in 1492
doesn't exactly provide you with what to do

when the love of your life leaves you,
or when you're left in the hallows of a
hospital room—

you leave emptier than you came,
but that's not what they tell you.
Soul, spread wide to a sterile ceiling—begging
to any God, that he might let you keep this
Life you carry in the meadows of your
being—
a love greater than any you've ever known.
I wish they taught us different subjects in
school—
Like how to grieve a life you never had—
to derive from an equation what it is like to
have a dad that wanted you—more than
temptation, careless whispers through his
phone,
a double drunk shot of whiskey on the
rocks—

you leave your interactions emptier than you
came,
but he tells you he's tired.
He's stressed and just a strung out mess,

having to provide for you is a chore but
darling I just adore you—
you didn't ask for this, for any of it—
for life, liberty or the pursuit of happiness,
but to my knowledge you're born into it
and once you're here, far be it to anyone to
blame you for something you had no say—
and the forbid the Heavens for blessing you
with the right to breathe and live just the
same—
life, liberty and happiness
that I so selfishly took from my father the day
he decided to be a father,
be a father,
be a father.

I wish they taught us different subjects in
school—
How to process that your womb was taken
from you by God and every good-for-nothing
person that came after him,
wasted your heart and time and love like they
could—
you leave emptier than you came,
down a bottle, down a dad, down a child,

you never met.

Journal Entry #2

I do not know all that I have written, but it
knows me—
better than the back of a hand,
or the bend of a gravel road that winds the
same way that it always has,
always will—
I pray that it is taken by me,
the same way that I am taken by a breeze,
moved to tears by a foreign prophet, call Him
Elohim—
let my consciousness stream—
can you see the motif?
the underlying theme I have woven into
seams,
the fabric of a daydream—
my hands in her hair,
a clandestine affair—
whispers for forgiveness on the end of a
prayer,
sung in a language we all can hear,
and with that fear, disappears—
and I am taken by it,

the same way dying spend their last breath on
a smile,
as if they have come to understand everything
worthwhile—
and with breath, goes any thought of exile,
for He who passes Judgement was once the
subject of judgement too,
and still had the forethought to bare you—
and I am taken by it.

"Why Do You Write?"

I often find myself caught up in the
paradigms of poetry,
sonically spellbound by sonnets and
villanelles and the ways their syllables ring to
my ears like church bells—they always gave
me a home, even when the four walls of my
own seemed to be made of fractured glass—
my parents always thought it was 'one way',
the kind where they could see in, but we
couldn't see out,
the same way my father treated their vows,
my mother had to stay in while he stepped
out—

I was 14 the first time I took a knife to my
skin—
told my mother that I didn't like him, she
didn't listen—
but then again, how could she, when she
couldn't see in?

my brothers and I watching the silence
suffocate the two of them,

our ears pressed to a builder's grade door
frame,
it's there that I learned poetry for the first
time and my brothers learned that not talking
had to be better than talking like this,
a habit they will probably never kick—

we get branded as antisocial, wiser than our
years—
but is that just something adults say because
it's easier than admitting that they cannot see
in either,
and they know that maturity in a 5-year-old
has to come from somewhere other than
chocolate milk, Kraft Mac and Cheese, and
gas station slushies—

the kinds of stains only your mother could get
out of your favorite t-shirt,
your father doesn't understand why that
matters,
you and your brothers have plenty of t-shirts
and he should know—
he goes to work and slaves away every day to
feed you, cloth you, do all of the things that

you need him to do because you can do
anything for yourself—

"you need to learn to be a man's son, stand on
your own two feet and make something of
yourself, I won't let a kid with a bad
handshake out of this house, and so help me
God if you and your sister don't clean up after
yourselves—you won't embarrass me, waste
my time, my money—can't you see that I'm
stressed— Stand up straight, you look like
you're carrying a backpack full of
weights—keep playing like that and no one
will ever want you, you can be damn sure of
that"—

No one ever bothers to tell him that he's right
or wrong,
it's in their silence that it's acknowledged,
so we learn to bleed better,
punish ourselves for being children and
wanting to do childish things,
like play with our imaginary friends or sink
into a Netflix binge—

those things were easier than body building
and pretending that our mother never cried,

she thought that she never let us see but I
know she cried because I saw it with my own
eyes when she first found out that my father
was making plans to share his nights with
someone else,
but God, I know those clandestine
conversations didn't start or end there—
I was a child, but wise beyond my years in
knowing how patterns work,
and that my father was not capable of loving
any one thing for a lifetime,
me, my mother, and my family.

He wants to talk about it now— fixing it- the
distance,
but doesn't want to look our gaping wounds
in the eyes,
see the kids on the other side of the glass that
worked just fine the whole time,
because then he might have to admit that he
installed it wrong,

put it in backwards, liked things on the
outside because they never made him look in,
at the home he created,
and then beat damn near to death,
with a vigor, and venom,
that those of us who are wise—know spells
resent.

My mother, my brothers and I are afraid of
the dark, loud noises and the sound of house
keys in the backdoor—
a lock turns over
my brothers disappear from the living room
me and my mother are left to brave it,
he asks how my day is, and thinks that
somehow this paper-thin conversation is
absorbent enough to the bare the weight of
all he has said, all he has done—
will somehow sop up the blood and the tears
and the vomit, that comes with having to
learn every day that you grew up with a single
mom, and lived in a house of fucking mirrors
that your father built to look at himself—

maybe he put it up right all along.

It is clear to me now why I am so taken by the
paradigms of poetry—
the structure of a sonnet, the music within a
villanelle—meter built up around me, like the
bricks of the home my family always
deserved—
peace comes in realizing that my father will
never learn,
and that he certainly doesn't understand the
concept that his children didn't ask to be
birthed—
but rest assured they know their father breaks
things,
and still expect something in return.

"Tell Me About Ryan"

I let you paint my face in strokes of saw grass
blades in the summertime,
I was allergic—
so were you, but how were we supposed to
know?
We were chasing fireflies through the fields in
the setting sunlight sublime,
and like dreams, we set them free, before
dark— a light show—
mason jars with screwdriver punched holes
that read in braille
an epic adventure of us,
the smell of outside and a friendship that
spans the test of time,

I drew parallel lines,
took up the space on a crinkled computer
paper page
until I realized I had fashioned myself a home,
four sides, and roof with room for you and
me and me and you—

You took me many places, just the same as I
took you,
the edge of the world on a wooden swing set,
my hat on backwards the way dad wore his,
and you with a paper-towel roll telescope,
taking in the world the way that it was always
meant to be.

I remember those days better than I know my
own name,
when a summer breeze sneaks through a crack
in my windowpane suddenly I am standing in
the face of a setting sun,
a bed sheet,
fashioned a cape waving so slightly behind
me—
I re-tie yours so it stays better, like mine—

We could have been anyone we wanted in the
moments, but you wanted me—
to fix your cape the way I did mine—to you it
must have looked right—
a status symbol I could have never
understood,

I let you paint my face in strokes of saw grass
blades in the summertime,
many summertimes, and I would have done it
all my life—
battling demons in the flicker of bonfire light,
our shadows dancing on the poolside—
the waltz of life,

Thank you for teaching me what it means for
someone to matter,
what I cannot live without,
and the ways of so many worlds—doors that
never close,
like the way they do when a breeze blows in,
I relive them over again

Journal Entry #3

Where were you,
and why do I keep asking questions I know
the answers to?
Maybe I didn't want you to tell me the truth—
say instead that you planned on pulling
through but got stuck waiting for your
feelings
to catch up with the rest of you,
so, you spent the night uptown going down
on someone who had an hourglass physique
and an affinity for liquor stronger than me—
but no,
nothing that extreme
you just fell out of love with me
and I could see it in the way you started to
silently put yourself to sleep
called out for an old lover when you were
dreaming—
I ask, "where were you",
not because you didn't come through,
you always did,
but your heart wasn't with you

"How About Your Mother?"

Dear You,
You— I've already picked out your name and
I'm only 22,
and I'm far from pregnant but so enchanted
to meet you.

Eager eyes and a bright smile, trust me,
with your tiny fingers in mine to guide you
through this life.
Afterall, I've learned from the best—
through the way my mother sat up and patted
my back,
taught me about life and death and how to
say a prayer when this life takes your breath,
my dear I've watched the woman take a
sledgehammer off the knee times three
just to pick it up and swear that "this won't
get the best of me" —
not for her but for me,
my brothers too,

and it's moments like these that made me,
changed the way I see adversity—
I want you to have that kind of love from me,
a gift that always allowed me to believe—
to dream, to have a heart that vowed to break
a glass ceiling,
she bore that in me.

My dear I've watched her stitch a baby
blanket till her fingers bled just so I could
close my eyes and go to bed,
make a patch for my pocket in the form a
promise to never be too far out of my reach
when kindergarten tears soaked my cheeks—
I still carry that patch from time to time,
doubt she knows that but I want you to know
that I will make you promises too,
the way my mom taught me to, with meaning
in my words and your precious heart in my
hands,
I vow to always give your head a place to land
My dear she's said it in a million languages my
whole life—

"This will always be your home, no matter
how far you go, you can come back, never
have to ask"
even at this age, I still rest my head on her
chest and feel a bond unlike anything I've
ever experienced,
a home in a home where I want to take you
back to,
show you the walls that made me and let
them help shape you too.

My dear the two of us have gone through
Things,
seen the beautiful and the stupid and the
in-between,
but I promise you it has most certainly been
something to see—
a people knocked down 100 times just to get
back up 101 because every battle can be won.

Maybe that's beautiful,
or stupid, but for both our sakes I hope it's
something in-between,
because your mama doesn't like too stupid or
too beautiful—

extremes have never really been this family's
thing,
my mom raised me on moderation,
not too high not too low,
"a level head makes good decisions, rises to
occasions", stands steady in windbreak.

And that is my wish for you my dear,
to teach you all that my mom taught me,
stand tall in the face of adversity,
fall in love with the beautiful and the stupid
and the in-between,
always know you have a place to rest your
head on me,
arms to carry you home, no matter how far
you go, and a love to show you all that you
can be.

Journal Entry #4

"Tell me about your day",
you say,
in the glow of a fish tank light
and to the lullaby of white noise—
I remember you this way and always will,
no matter how life paints me black and blue
I promise to remember you
in every stage of being you,
the you in a fish tank light, Jusko's Tee—
shirt green—
I will be here,
remembering you,
even when you cannot remember me.

Journal Entry #5

I will always love poetry more than you ever
loved me,
and for that, I am grateful—
to know a love with no bounty,
as benevolent and as wise
as I need,
when I need it—
to know that любовь and love are one in the
same,
and you will never know любовь,
its depths and the ways that it moves me—
something else you have made the conscious
decision to lose—
another reason I am sad for you.
I suppose it should come as no surprise that
your favorite color is blue,
and hobbies include longing for places that
you already knew,
and a hatred for me—
all that I do,
but I swear to you that I will never say sorry
that I flew—

spent a lifetime working to undo this fucked
up worldview
you are so certain to be true—
too afraid to pursue the meaning of your
tattoo—
cut it off.

I'll never share something with someone I
outgrew.

Progress Report: Headspace

Now a-days I find myself frequently starved
of inspiration,
malnourished,
like life has bled me dry,
leeched all my passion,
and poured it to the stark ground, where I
prepare for burial,
giving back to the giver of life is something I
never thought I'd have to see in black and
white,
but truth is, I'm tired.
And I think that I have been tired for a long
time—

it shows on the undersides of my eyes as I live
every day watching my own life pass me by—
No one asks if I'm fine—
they know I'm not,
and asking just puts us both in a weird spot,

    I have to lie,

    and they have to pretend to be blind—

so instead, we keep our conversations light—
ask each other about the weather, and if we
saw the Tiger's game last night—
The thought of baseball makes me want to
vomit, but I always loved the sound of metal
cleats,
if I close my eyes, I can fantasize about
someone running,
across my back—beating and bleeding my
skin until I get feeling back—
                        climax—

You ask if I did,
and I don't lie so I tell you yes,
always being careful to leave out the why,

because now a-days people ask too many
fucking questions that they don't want, or
already know, the answers to,
-        have you been crying?
-        yes
-        do you love her?
-        yes
-        do you hate me?
-        yes

I always heard that the truth will set you free,
but who ever said that doesn't know me—
or doesn't really know what it means to be
free,
honesty has always been the slowest kind of
death for me.

It's the kind that leads me here,
to barren ground,
soulless, searching for feeling in a God
forsaken pit,
waiting to be found,
the winter wind gales,

and I,
read your letters in grayscale,

                              -do you hate

me?

                              -yes
                              -do you love

her?

                              -yes
                              -have you

been crying?

                              -yes,
                                the truth

will set you free.
        Now pick up your shovel,

                fucking bury me.

"What Happened With Her?"

You told my mother, you only ever wanted me
to choose you,
so, consider this poem my way to defuse the
narrative that I would never choose you—
because here I am,
choosing you,
after all of this time,
despite all of the lies,
and fact that your worth to me has died—
choosing to take up space,
on a page,
to tell you that choosing you was the smallest
mistake I have ever made—
smallest, because I've made bigger walking
around with an untied shoe than I ever made
when it came to you,
wasted my time,
lied until I no longer knew you—
I never did.

I've made mistakes with more deliverance,
stubbing my toe on a wooden stool with more
backbone that you could have mustered—
this poem has more structure,
more discipline,
than any practice you invest your life in—
I hope it kills you—
metaphorically speaking, that my words paint
you truer than anything you could ever do,
I hope this finds you,
and you realize that me,
choosing you,
will be the most noteworthy thing to ever
happen to you.

Journal Entry #6

My open letter to you, Darling, will one day
end,
when some stranger's lips breathe life into
me—
teach me to love again,
but until then,
may you find me in all of the things you love
and love them a little less,
always having to think of my benevolence—I
digress,
conclude that my love was too true for you—
who much preferred my body and the things
you wanted to make it do—
I trusted you—
I'm the rock in the sole of your running shoes.
The author of a catchphrase you over use,
the taste in your mouth that follows every
excuse—
abuse the people in this life that loved you for
who they thought they knew—
baby, I will always be your greatest muse.

One day I will leave all of these letters to you,
when I am writing for someone new,
and you, and your baby blues will be nothing
more than words on a page,
a girl with no name,
my poetry career being your 15 seconds of
fame—
say my name.
Say it twice,
taste every syllable,
my every vice, inadmissible—
they will say of your crimes,
until my pen—
biblical,
can recreate a story so fucking formidable—
visible,
to every person who ever dared open their
mouth unprepared to swallow the poison of a
promise,
coated in Judas' varnish—
add that to the list of happenings I'd like to
admonish,
but for now, I will keep admonishing you—

should have just let me be the rock in your
running shoes
the spider in your room,
the reason you cannot listen to "Maroon"—
because I promise you will rue what you
pursue,
I will run through you.
I pray you never have to encounter the
version of me
birthed after you,
she feels no sympathy for you—
hopes you choke on the words of a person she
thought she knew,
and how they taste like glass—
cut out your tongue, render you mute,
use the shards to peel away the mask—
ask if she cares—
she doesn't.
To her this is medicinal, clinical—
extracting a parasite from its host,
it's engrossed in all of the parts of you she
hated most—
why couldn't you leave well enough alone?

Now you are going to atone,

welcome home.

"How Do You Feel About Her Now?"

I never missed you.

And the poem could end there,
uncomfortably simple,
like we did—

but I think I'll drag it out,
like you did to me—
tell you how deeply I loved you, and how I
found myself grief sick when the mask
slipped—
but that would be a lie—
your territory,
not mine—
so I'll tell you the truth,
that my mind's eye always saw you,
knew that your laundry was dirty,
despite the spin cycle you put us through—
was I supposed to believe that she didn't
touch you?

Two hours is too long to ghost someone you
call home—
blowing up your phone,
I knew you were walking alone—

what I didn't know was that your back was
being broken into the same hand-me-down
mattress that watched me show up
unannounced with flowers and strawberry
wine—
I wish it could have seen your face instead of
having to pity mine—
should have known the look in your eyes was
fear,
not surprise,
and the more I think about it, the more it
keeps me up at night
how could I have missed the signs?
when you opened that door, you expected to
see Sydney's face,
not mine.

I hope that one day you read this, and it
makes you cry—

I leave you with the actuality that much to
your dismay,
Sydney and I happen to get along just fine—
we both like strawberry wine
and plotting about people that crossed a
line—

consider this our kiss of death,
this poem Sydney commissioned me to write
from her,
and from me—
let you know that we are beauty,
and you are everything we built you to be—
individuality is something you could never
perceive,
so I pray you succeed,
and always see me

"Tell me About Leo"

To the man that I always needed my father to
be,
I think watching you grow is what healed
me—
born on December 13th,
if I'm being honest,
between me and these notebook leaves,
he's the only man I'll ever say that I need—

Our story started with his 'serious face
onesie',
And a two-step country tune,
that now, he would turn his nose up to—
"Days Go By",
they certainly do,
I'd be lying if I said that I didn't get choked
up at the thought of you--

I never knew that taking care of you would be
what set me free
from an absence I felt deep in my being—
when you hug me,
you have always fit perfectly,
in the parts of me that were missing

To the man I always needed my father to be
thank you for endlessly reflecting
on things other than your own reflection,
taking time to see that our mirrors were
two-way,
and with that, the responsibility that came--
you are gentle
warm
kind
and have always given the best advice,
"follow your heart, unless it hurts,
nothing like that is worth it"
still rings in my mind
and I promise every day, for you I try,
because days go by,
like a country tune
how quickly you grew

into the man I always needed my father to
be—
you are the only man I will ever need,
I hope you are proud of me

Progress Report:
Progress?

how long have I been sitting here,
chained to this desk by the heart on my sleeve
and that old leather-bound book where I used
to write your name,
like dandelion seeds on a summer breeze—
how far do they go,
and let's go,
back to another time
with him and I
chasing dandelion puffs through barnyard
grass in summertime,
he digs a swarm of gnats out of your eye
lashes
to the backdrop of a firestorm sunset
and chase—
chase after that—
like his voice, when it rolls in on a
thunderclap
and brings the smell of rain to wash out a
long day,

his memory will always take me to the same
place—
my little brother on my hip,
my 7-year-old arms try hard not to let him
slip—
we danced, and stay dancing,
to a Keith Urban song that so melodically
sings to my past—
I will always chase—
chase after that

Journal #7

I once read that history does not repeat itself
but rather informs—
do with that what you will,
but it brings me to the same place every
time—
knowledge is power,
and 'We the People' would rather repeat than
read—
the drag marks left in the sand by your
great-grandad,
Normandy Beach still bleeds,
no one leaves for free—

God would he be ashamed to see the tyranny
this country welcomed with open arms,
on our knees for a false prophet
with a vested interest in profit
and resurrecting rhetoric people died to
protect against—
do with that what you will,
but I refuse to stand mute in the boot prints
of my grandfather

and everyone that came before him that had
the courage to say—
and mean—
that all men were created equal,
in a way that is more than colloquial and
broader than any colonial
ever could have imaged—

we've been down this road before,
the story has been written so open your
fucking eyes and listen—
history does not repeat,
it informs,
knowledge is power—
and under this regime,
I can assure you,
even the loyal,
won't leave for free—
"Under the spreading chestnut tree,
I sold you,
and you sold me"

"How Are You Today?"

The drama of it all was written 10,000 years
ago in Sanskrit,
and then written, and written over again,
like the bend of a willow's branch,
leaves stroking the Earth,
soft, methodical–
intentioned
is the speed, of a steady breeze and a mind
run amuck
with the poison you secrete, words roll off
your pen–
your tongue– the sharpest weapon,
is who I've become,
evanesce when her pinned up hair comes
undone–
honey-soaked highlights, blush in the rays of
sunshine,
and I am rendered breathless, bewildered
beyond all sense and sensation I can
understand;
I wonder if she can understand me,
charmed, like a serpent to flute,

Eve to a pestilent fruit—
She could tell me 10,000 times it was poison,
and I'd still tend to her root,
soft, methodical–
intentioned
is a steady hand, that knows its place,
with the mastery of a craftsman,
on the side of her face, slips over her
waist--lowercase,
is the pace at which hearts should learn to
race–
in the distance,
a herd of horse hooves
is reduced to a rumble fainter than
thunder – the flutter of hummingbird wings,
leaves butterfly kisses on cheeks
and I can remember,
the drama of it all, wasn't drama at all

Journal Entry #8

I want you to know that I would look for you
in every life,
spend all my days,
eyes wide—
I promise to find you every time.

"Have You Tried a Pros and Cons List?"

- A memory—consciousness whispers a suggestion,
- where do you hide in daylight?
- I called for her, no answer
- the silence, like an open wound—
- quiet was heavy—it crushed us
- I lose my breath—it's realized,
- the writing stops, a hollow exhale—
- count on me, not your hands—
- true—as your mother speaks scripture
- the hills and I have eyes,
- why won't you look at me?
- Do you hate what you see?
- Too refined for short form poetry,
- daddy's little girl grows old—tired
- Logic tells you to bury her—
- bury her, 6 feet, down deep—
- underneath the boughs of cherry trees,
- you are the company you keep

- please—please just look at me—
- blood and benevolence know no bounty
- bountiful and beautiful—I stay bleeding
- dress the wound, or fields will—
- splayed to the sky, God cries—
- Look at me—please just look,
- Silence hurts—she shovels more dirt
- Baby, show me where it hurts?
- Covert hate kills just the same
- call the hearse—say my name
- maybe then she sees my face
- bountiful, beautiful, bleeding, dreaming— far away

Journal Entry #9

for the first time in my life,
I found myself unbothered by the fact that no
one seemed to find me,
I wasn't trying to hide,
but certainly wasn't trying to be something
that needed finding—
like car keys, or the life that used to live in
your parents' eyes—
they tell us everything is fine—
but I'm far too old to not know the difference
between fine and formidable.
It's interlaced in the way they do things—
my mother,
existing so quietly that he never sees her,
and my father,
so loud,
so boisterous,
it's all she can perceive.
It's like a pressure cooker—the top vibrating
from the heat.
They tell us things used to be better, but from
what I can remember,

Things have always just been fine—
or formidable—
whichever,
because I'm far too old to not know that they
are interchangeable

"Have You Been in Love?"

tell me where you are
and why you spend all this time
trying to hide from me—
and I,
trying to find you,
have spent countless nights with a lantern
cast out from my side
as a wicker wick burns—
guides my sight—
yet after these nights
you seem to be the only thing that is left to
find—
this heart of mine,
full of poetry sonnets
has been admonished by not so platonic
promises
made in the in-betweens of my sheets
the interlay of the secrets we keep,
memories of your mystique,
ethereal enough to make me weep—

my hands give oblique suggestions for the
words we cannot speak,
we do what we do best until we fall asleep—
and you, with an errant hair cast over your
cheek, could not be more picturesque—
sun rays sneak along your shoulder blades and
paint them gold
through the breast of an open window,
in this light God draws you both delicate and
bold—
your amber eyes flutter and entomb me
you know I am ready to die here,
enchanted to live the rest of my life here
with you and the summertime sun
casting soft shadows everywhere my hands
have been—
incandescent finger paints
trace your curves and edges
and cover you completely in the beauty
I see—you smile at me

there is no place I'd rather be

Journal #10

I promised her that one of these days I would
be bigger than the whole sky,
and I meant it– the way a child means it
when they say 'I love you'
or when a mother tells you she is
disappointed–
intentioned– pointed,
a compass to the North,
will always give way
to those that ask to be anointed
for their transgressions– procrastinations and
hyper fixations–
Mother Nature displays in interlays and sky
brushed fingerpaints,
the colors she sets ablaze,
on a summer's moonlit haze–
proves to us that she owns the whole sky
and nothing you try
can ever be as impossible,
as seeing rainbows at night.

"Tell Me About Mallorie"

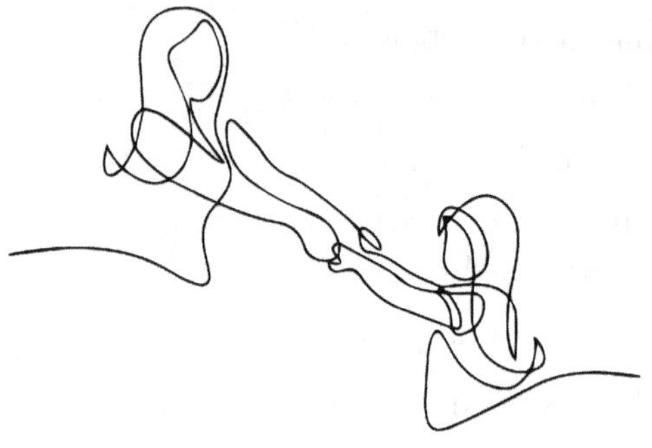

You asked me to write a poem about you,
and my friend
that's something I never thought you'd ask me
to do—

and let me tell you,
for someone who doesn't like to share their
shades of blue, you have certainly entrusted
me with a few—and when it comes to you, I
promise to delve into any hue—in fact, you
have made me quite sensitive to blue, and the
ways it changes on you—
something you'd say my eyes could never do—
You asked me to write a poem about you,

and my friend
that's something I never thought you'd ask me
to do—

                              because
you know that I am secretly sentimental,
something I keep close to my chest,
padlocked—the key tossed away through
time, into a 1992 community pool—
you can breathe underwater, retrieving it was
an easy task for you, the other kids were
shocked you hadn't gone blue, but had they
just listed maybe they too would have the
privilege of understanding you—
A latchkey,
that fit every lock in every door, in every
town, in every lifetime she lived—lighting up
rooms with vigor and truth– an undeniable
fire has always burned in you—stronger than
the ocean, than a river, than a man—
                    to say I wish I had
known you then—

            but I suppose I did,
You carried that key for me, none the wiser,

under the water, where you could breathe,
along hundreds of hours of highways, spring
break hide-aways, the top of a hand-me down
dresser that I shared with your hamsters cage,
through every door of every place you called
home, in the front pocket of your first winter
coat, the cup holder of your car the day you
finally drove away—decided that your life
didn't need to be something that made you
afraid—
You asked me to write a poem about you,
and my friend
that's something I never thought you'd ask me
to do—
because I don't have to write to you for you to
know that you have always been seen by me,
the eldest child in me sees through the
smokescreen, to the ache that sulks in the
blue of your eyes when you remember the
back seat of your mom's 1988—the nights
were long, but she kept you safe,
and when you talk about her, I watch your
chest inflate,
she lives in you,

the same way I watch you live in everything
you do—
You asked me to write a poem about you,
and my friend
that's something I never thought you'd ask me
to do—

                          because you
know that I love you,
love you more than I can ever truly explain,
and that's something I have always struggled
to say, in the hairpins of conversation and
casualties of the day to day—but truth of the
matter is, I am always happy to see you, and
live in the worlds we managed to create—
thank you, for always lighting up a room,
showing me how to love the color blue, and
carrying a key—taking care of me, long before
I could breathe, I thank God that you always
knew how—
underwater,
in the backseat of a 1988,
you did and do,
burn brighter than anyone I ever knew

Journal #11

I met a girl in a dream that was far more alive
than I will ever be—
I can't be too sure,
but I think that is fine with me—
my definition of 'alive' has changed damn
near a million times
but I think I've settled on something that is
easy
and regular and fine,
and there is nothing wrong with easy or
regular or fine
as long as you are fine
laying your head on her chest at night,
using the count of her heartbeats to tell the
time—
everything about her is beautiful
and easy and regular and fine—
it's been a lifetime since a woman has kept me
up at night,
for good or bad or otherwise,

for her I'll re-read Gertrude Stein—

"Bundles For Them"
a lovely poem
that used to be all mine
before I opened my heart to Perfidy and Judas
and let them twist the knife
while I read aloud
a message written for the love of my life,
turns out easy and regular and fine
rarely happens at the same time—
but I know the pieces fit just right when I
show Jess a picture of her and I—
her smile barely fits under her eyes
she tells me it's fine to melt when I see her,
and actually, more regular
than anything I've done in a long time,
and that my smile and the way her hands
reach for me,
looks easy,
like it was meant to be,
and I think that's more than fine with me—
maybe even lovely...

Hermeneutic

I scheduled my first appointment when I
found myself chasing a shadow—
wondering where we went when we fell
asleep,
tucking myself in,
wondering what it would be like to really
have a friend
that loved me the way my brothers always
did—
chasing fireflies and song lyrics about our
days going by
and not once stopping to think
what that actually meant—

I only ever wanted a child because of the
childhood they gave me,
I will never need another friend as long as we
always walk in threes,
a gift my mother gave to me—
I keep them close,
tattooed on my chest,
coast to coast,
they have made me realize that
I never missed you—
that is true
and I think I knew
I was better when I could write your name in
my poetry again—
say to hell with you Annie
and to hell with that God damn ring
I would sooner fashion myself jewelry with
my own shoestrings—
be alone until my flesh melts through my
bones
than ever build another home
made of mirrors—
where my father taught me that любовь
was something that you could choose
when it's convenient for you—

I know love when my mother,
my brothers,
look to me
and I knew I was better
when I accepted that was all I'd ever need—
sunsets in summertime
days go by,
you all are the loves of my life.